HAL•LEONARD®

GUITAR PLAY-ALONG

AUDIO ACCESS INCLUDED

PLAYBACK+
Speed • Pitch • Balance • Loop

VOL. 6

'90s ROCK

To access audio visit:
www.halleonard.com/mylibrary

Enter Code
2138-3514-7162-1361

ISBN 978-1-5400-5904-8

HAL•LEONARD®

Visit Hal Leonard Online at
www.halleonard.com

Contact us:
Hal Leonard
7777 West Bluemound Road
Milwaukee, WI 53213
Email: info@halleonard.com

In Europe, contact:
Hal Leonard Europe Limited
42 Wigmore Street
Marylebone, London, W1U 2RN
Email: info@halleonardeurope.com

In Australia, contact:
Hal Leonard Australia Pty. Ltd.
4 Lentara Court
Cheltenham, Victoria, 3192 Australia
Email: info@halleonard.com.au

CONTENTS

Guitar Notation Legend

THE MUSICAL STAFF shows pitches and rhythms and is divided by bar lines into measures. Pitches are named after the first seven letters of the alphabet.

TABLATURE graphically represents the guitar fingerboard. Each horizontal line represents a string, and each number represents a fret.

4th string, 2nd fret

1st & 2nd strings open, played together

open D chord

HALF-STEP BEND: Strike the note and bend up 1/2 step.

WHOLE-STEP BEND: Strike the note and bend up one step.

GRACE NOTE BEND: Strike the note and immediately bend up as indicated.

SLIGHT (MICROTONE) BEND: Strike the note and bend up 1/4 step.

BEND AND RELEASE: Strike the note and bend up as indicated, then release back to the original note. Only the first note is struck.

PRE-BEND: Bend the note as indicated, then strike it.

VIBRATO: The string is vibrated by rapidly bending and releasing the note with the fretting hand.

PALM MUTING: The note is partially muted by the pick hand lightly touching the string(s) just before the bridge.

HAMMER-ON: Strike the first (lower) note with one finger, then sound the higher note (on the same string) with another finger by fretting it without picking.

PULL-OFF: Place both fingers on the notes to be sounded. Strike the first note and without picking, pull the finger off to sound the second (lower) note.

LEGATO SLIDE: Strike the first note and then slide the same fret-hand finger up or down to the second note. The second note is not struck.

SHIFT SLIDE: Same as legato slide, except the second note is struck.

TRILL: Very rapidly alternate between the notes indicated by continuously hammering on and pulling off.

TAPPING: Hammer ("tap") the fret indicated with the pick-hand index or middle finger and pull off to the note fretted by the fret hand.

NATURAL HARMONIC: Strike the note while the fret-hand lightly touches the string directly over the fret indicated.

PINCH HARMONIC: The note is fretted normally and a harmonic is produced by adding the edge of the thumb or the tip of the index finger of the pick hand to the normal pick attack.

TREMOLO PICKING: The note is picked as rapidly and continuously as possible.

VIBRATO BAR DIVE AND RETURN: The pitch of the note or chord is dropped a specified number of steps (in rhythm), then returned to the original pitch.

VIBRATO BAR SCOOP: Depress the bar just before striking the note, then quickly release the bar.

VIBRATO BAR DIP: Strike the note and then immediately drop a specified number of steps, then release back to the original pitch.

Additional Musical Definitions

 (accent)
- Accentuate note (play it louder).

 (staccato)
- Play the note short.

D.S. al Coda
- Go back to the sign (𝄋), then play until the measure marked "***To Coda***," then skip to the section labelled "**Coda**."

D.C. al Fine
- Go back to the beginning of the song and play until the measure marked "***Fine***" (end).

Fill
- Label used to identify a brief melodic figure which is to be inserted into the arrangement.

N.C.
- Harmony is implied.

- Repeat measures between signs.

- When a repeated section has different endings, play the first ending only the first time and the second ending only the second time.

Are You Gonna Go My Way

Words by Lenny Kravitz
Music by Lenny Kravitz and Craig Ross

to   save the day.   And   I won't leave un - til I'm   done.

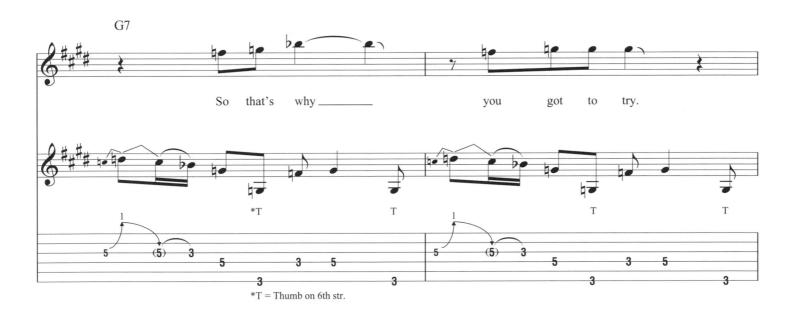

G7

So   that's   why _____   you   got   to   try.

*T = Thumb on 6th str.

You   got   to   breathe and   have some   fun.

Though I'm not paid, ___ I play this game. And I won't stop un - til I'm

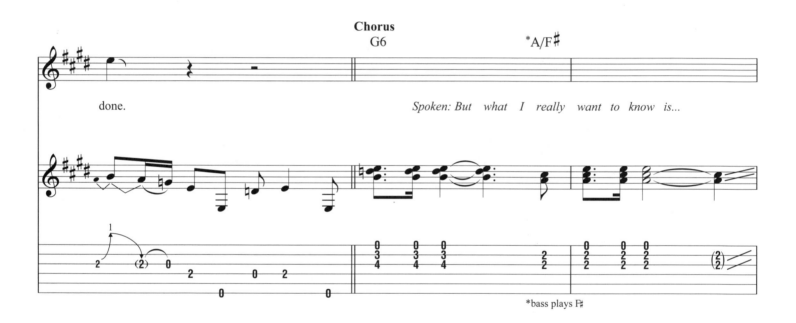

Chorus

done.

Spoken: But what I really want to know is...

*bass plays F♯

To Coda ⊕

Are you gon - na go my way?

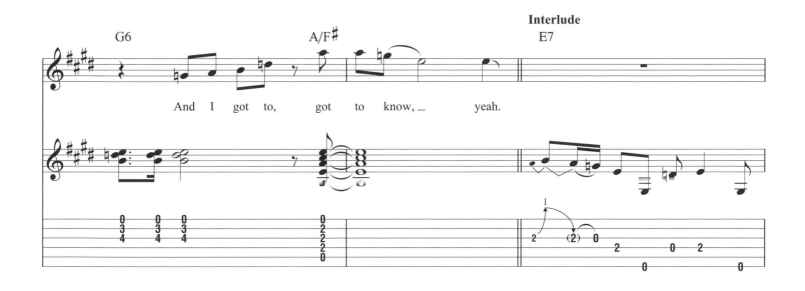

Interlude

And I got to, got to know, __ yeah.

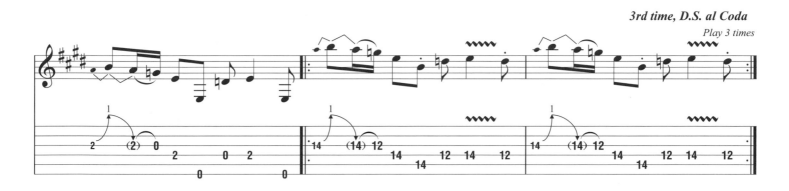

3rd time, D.S. al Coda

Play 3 times

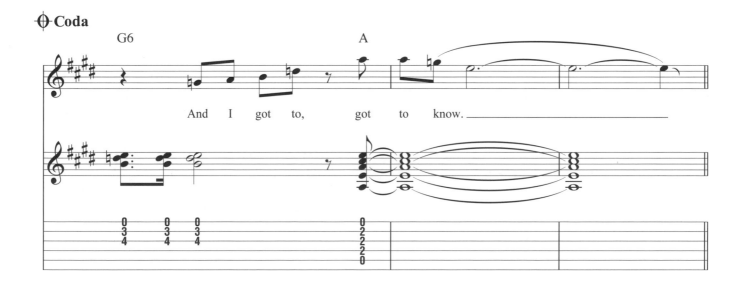

$\oplus$ **Coda**

And I got to, got to know. _____

Interlude   **Guitar Solo**

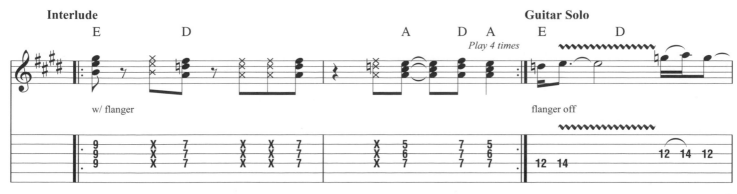

w/ flanger   flanger off

Play 4 times

9

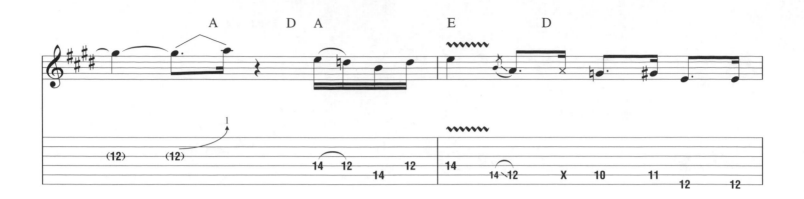

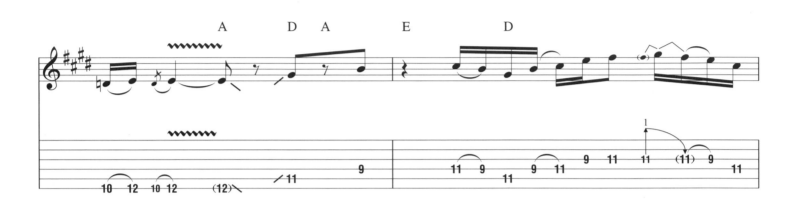

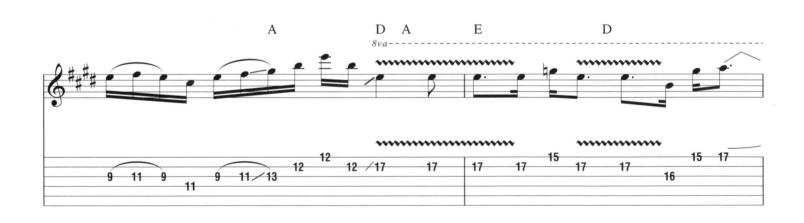

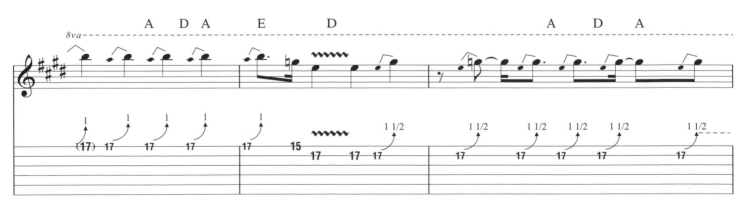

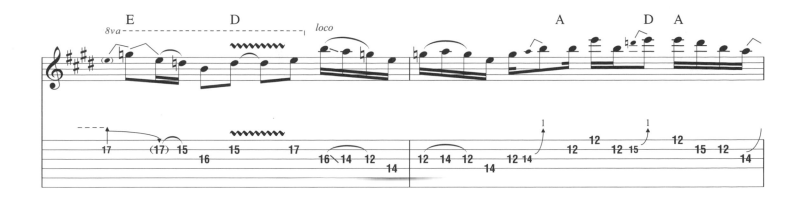

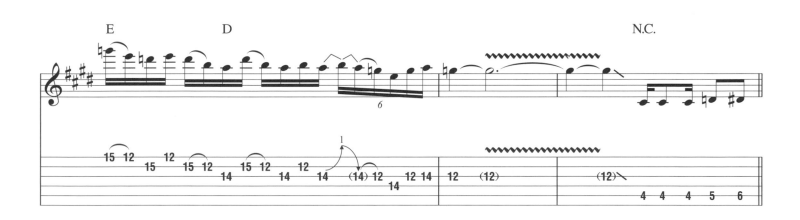

Interlude

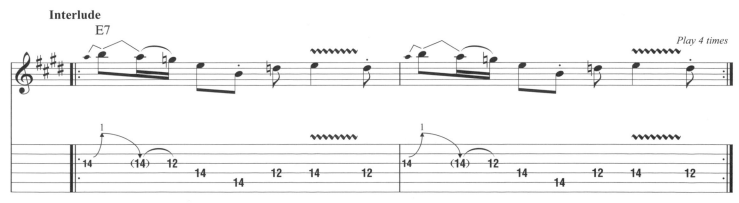

Outro-Chorus

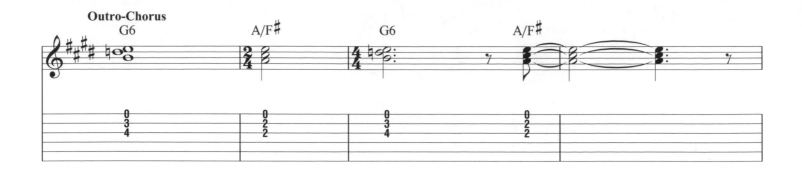

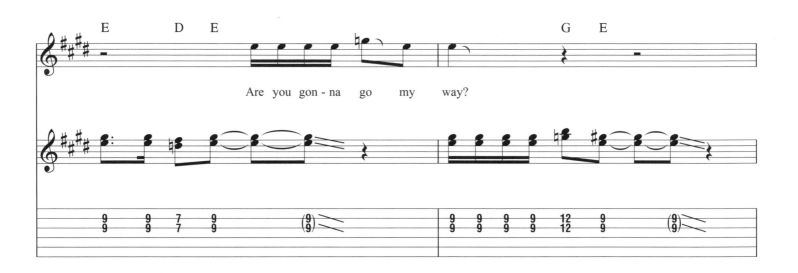

Are you gon-na go my way?

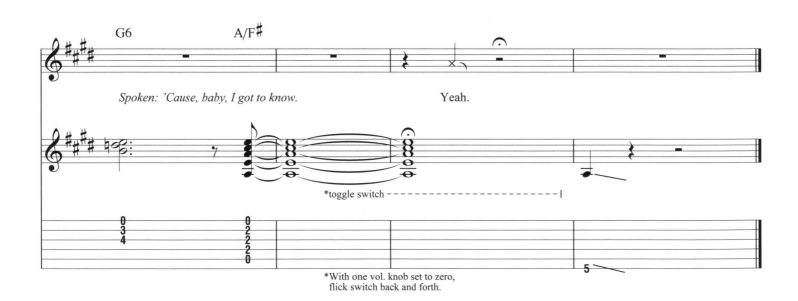

Spoken: 'Cause, baby, I got to know.   Yeah.

*toggle switch -|

*With one vol. knob set to zero,
flick switch back and forth.

Additional Lyrics

2. I don't know why we always cry.
   This we must leave and get undone.
   We must engage and rearrange
   And turn this planet back to one.
   So tell me why we got to die
   And kill each other one by one.
   We've got to hug and rub-a-dub.
   We've got to dance and be in love.

Killing in the Name

Written and Arranged by Rage Against The Machine

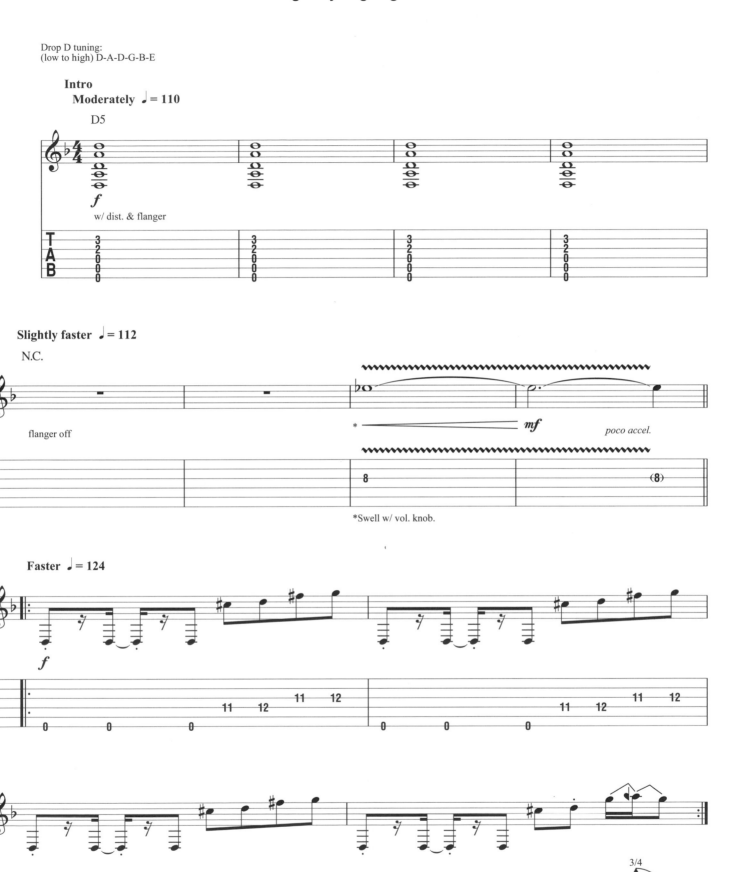

Slightly slower ♩ = 117

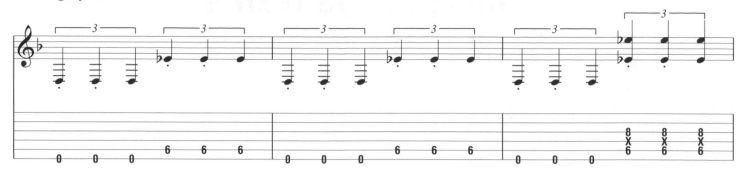

Slower ♩ = 82

N.C.(D5)

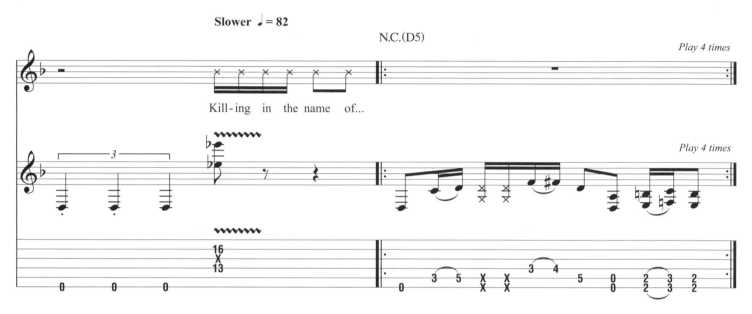

Kill-ing in the name of...

Play 4 times

Play 4 times

% Verse

N.C.(D5)

5th time, substitute Fill 1

Play 3 times

1., 2. Some of those _ that work forc - es   are the same _ that burn cross - es.

Play 3 times

slight P.M. - - - - ‖   slight P.M. - - - - - - - - - - - - - - - - ‖   slight P.M. - - - - - - - ‖

Fill 1

slight P.M. - - - ‖

Slightly faster ♩ = 93

And now you do what they told ___ ya.
And now you're un - der con - trol.

And now you do what they told ___ ya.
And now you're

And now you do what they told ___ ya.
un - der con - trol.

But now you do what they told ___ ya.
And now you're un - der con - trol. _____

Slightly slower ♩ = 89

Those who died ___ are jus - ti - fied ___ by wear-ing your badge ___ and your cho - sen white. You'll

jus - ti - fy ___ those that died ___ by wear-ing a badge ___ and your cho - sen white.

Guitar Solo

N.C.(D5)

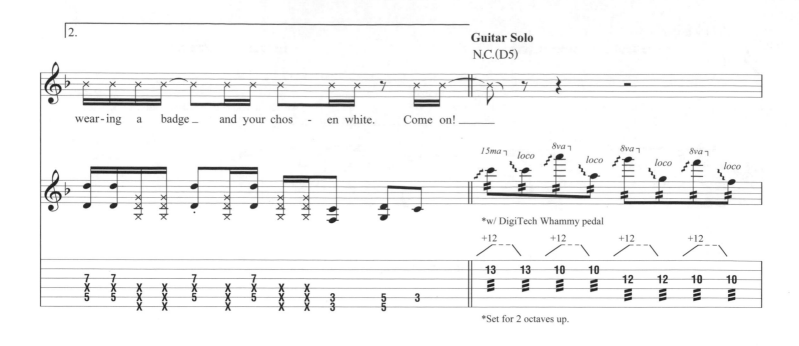

wear-ing a badge ___ and your chos - en white. Come on! _____

*w/ DigiTech Whammy pedal

*Set for 2 octaves up.

Lead Voc. w/ voc. ad lib, next 6 meas.

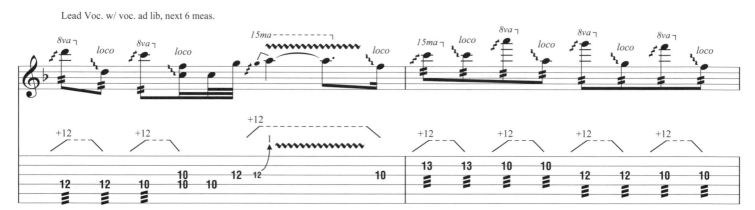

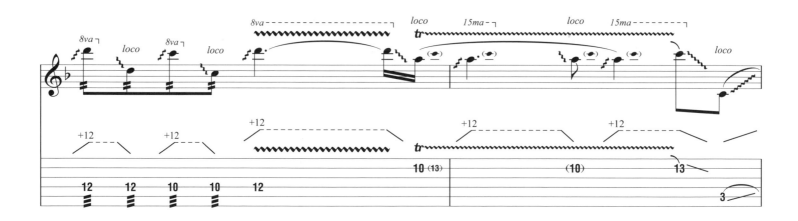

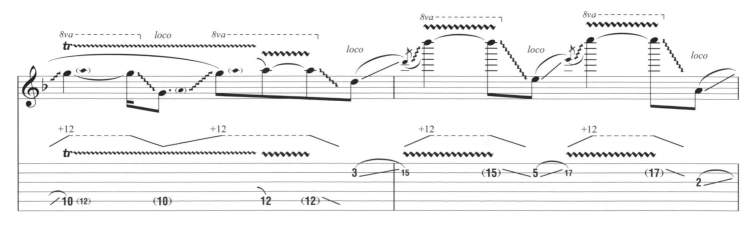

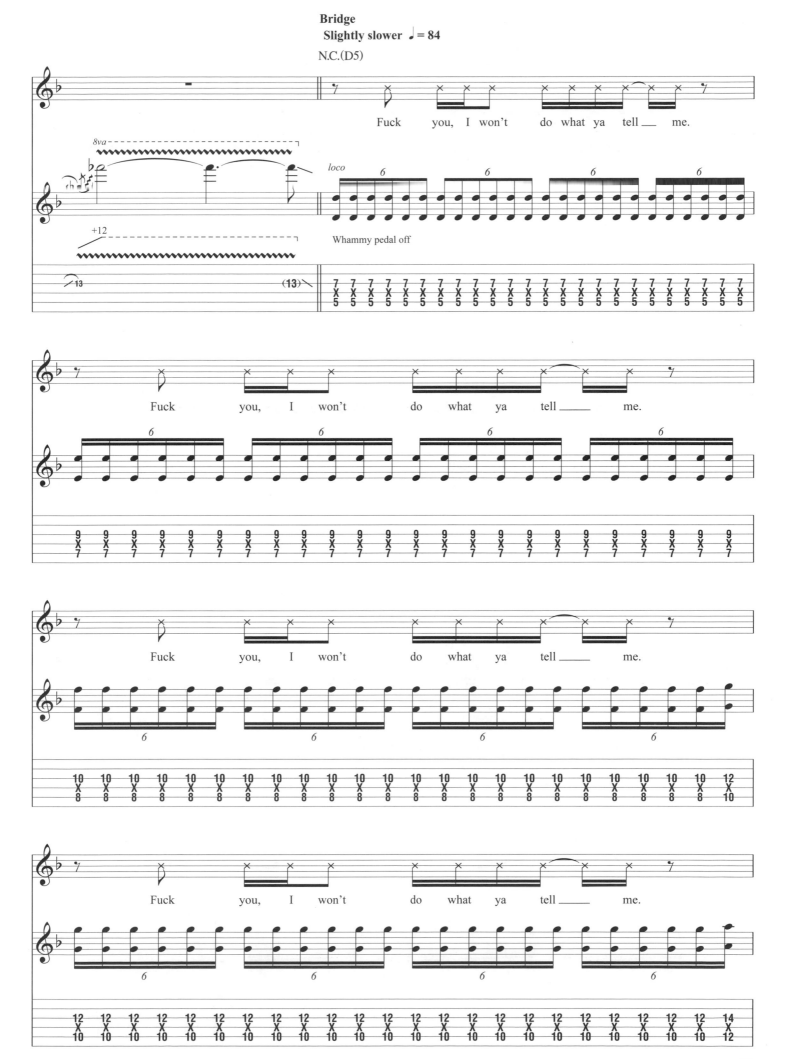

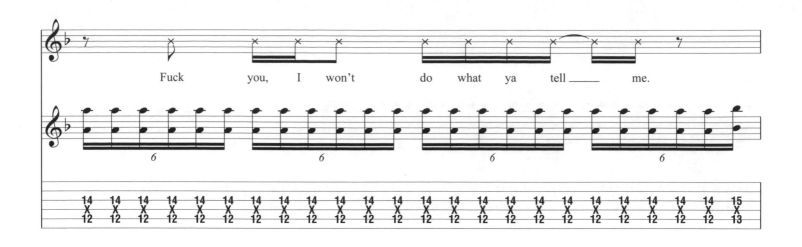

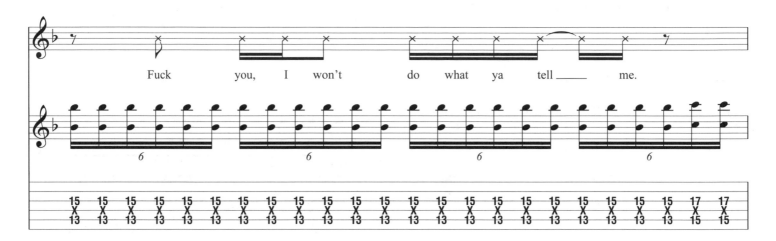

Slightly faster ♩ = 88

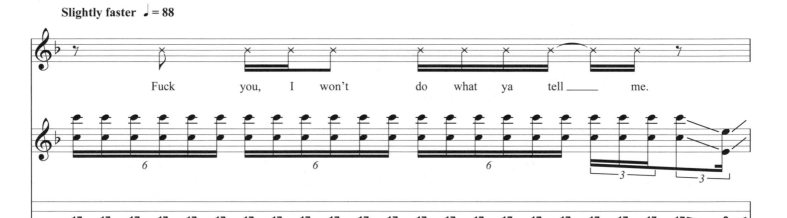

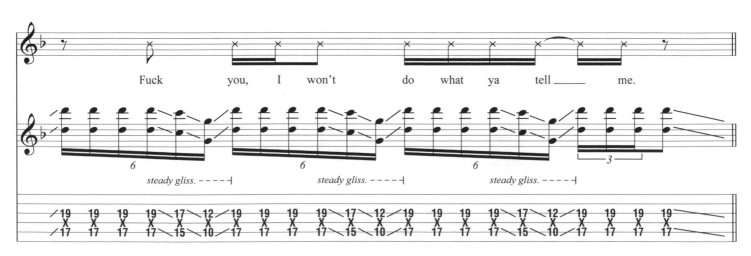

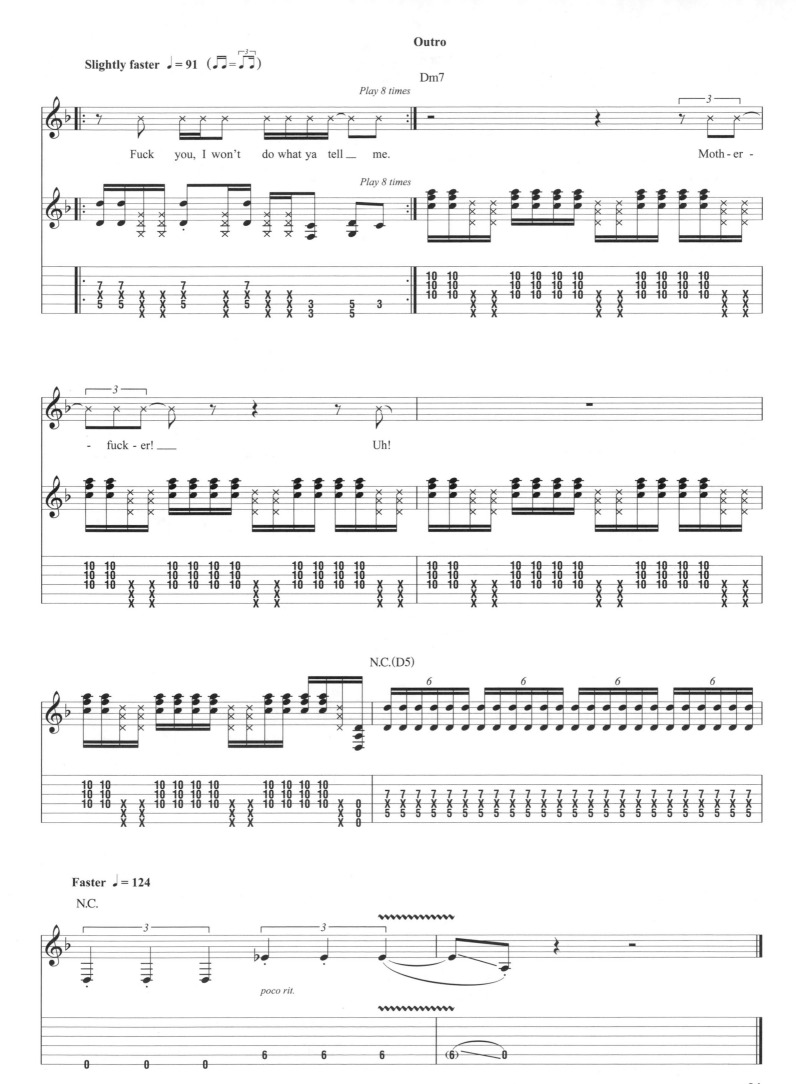

Creep

Words and Music by Albert Hammond, Mike Hazlewood, Thomas Yorke, Jonathan Greenwood, Colin Greenwood, Edward O'Brien and Philip Selway

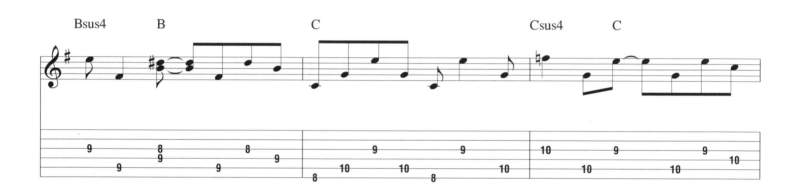

could-n't look you in the eye. _____ You're just like an an -

- gel.   (Your) skin makes me   cry. ____

You float like a feath - er _____ in a beau-ti-ful   world. __

I wish I was spe - cial.

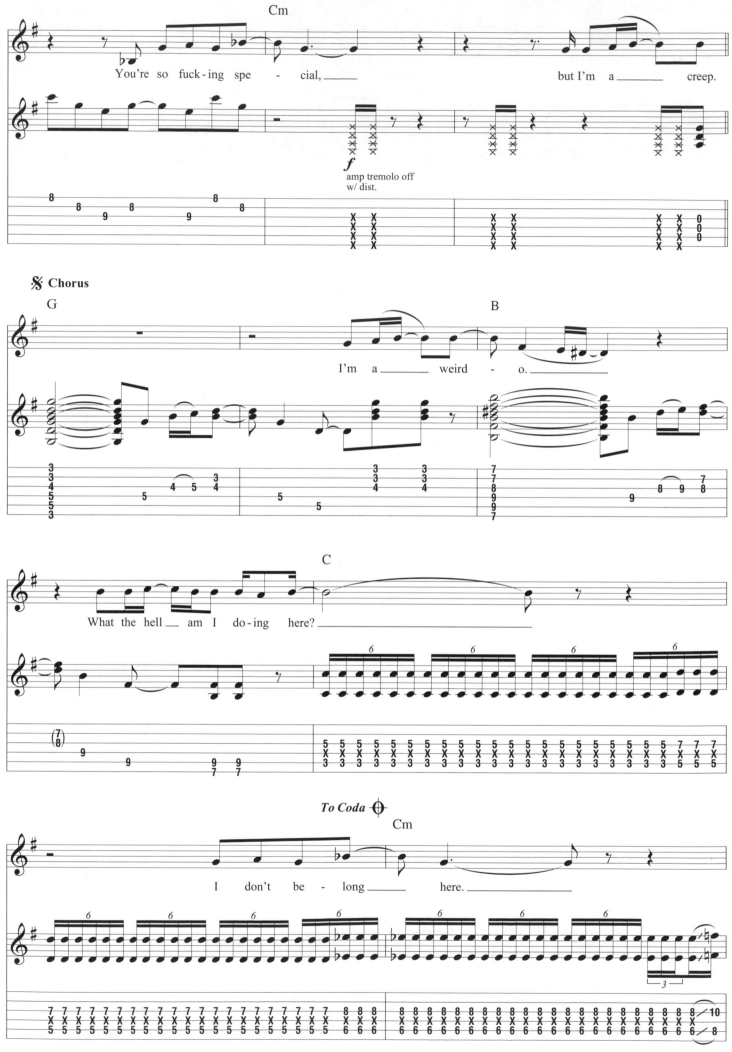

D.S. al Coda

Coda

Bridge

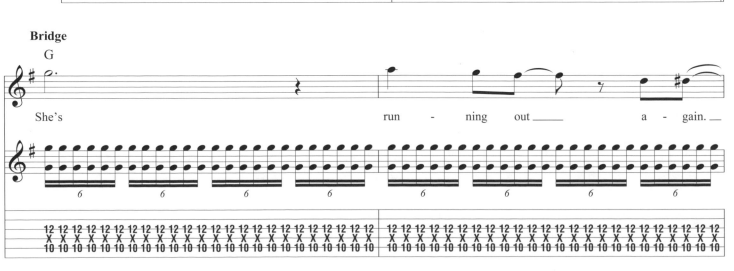

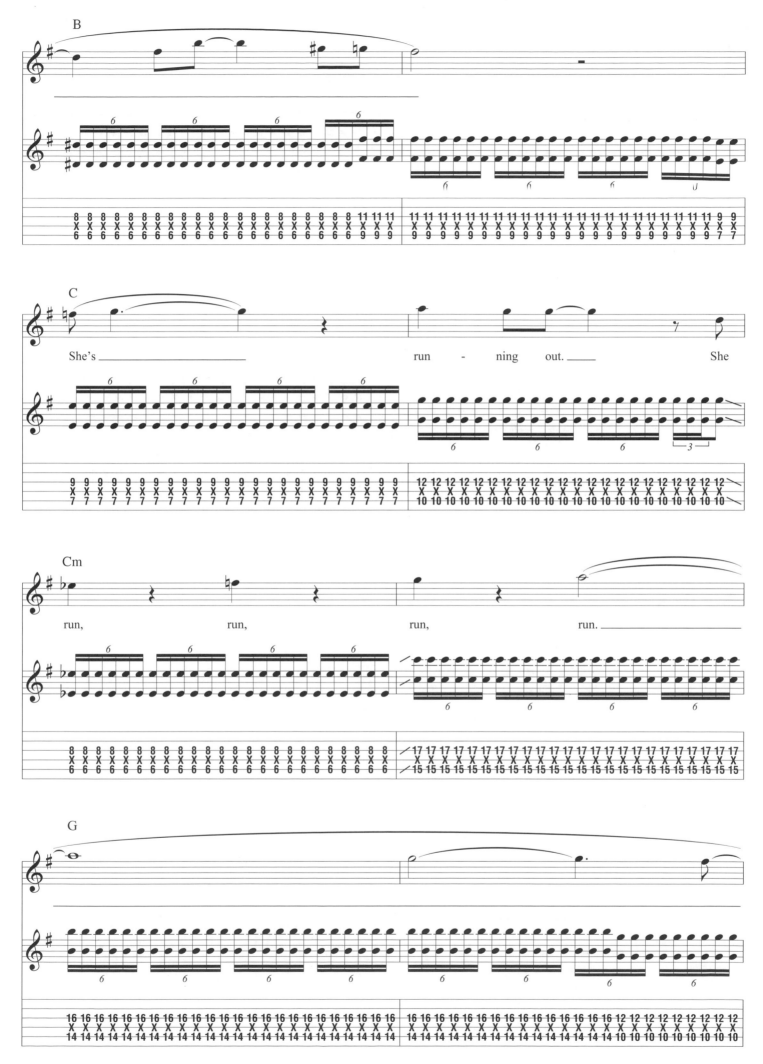

Loser

Words by Beck Hansen
Music by Beck Hansen and Karl Stephenson

Open D tuning:
(low to high) D-A-D-F#-A-D

Intro

Moderately ♩ = 85

Play 7 times

mf
w/ clean tone
w/ slide

1. In the

Verse

time of chim-pan-zees_ I was a mon-key. Bu-tane in my veins and I'm out to cut the junk-ie with the

w/ tremolo

Gtr. tacet

plas-tic eye-balls, spray paint the veg-'ta-bles. Dog food stalls with the beef-cake pan-ty-hose.

Kill the head-lights and put it in neu-tral. Stock car flam-ing with the los-er and the cruise con-trol.

Gtr. tacet

Ba-by's in Re - no with the vi - ta - min D.   Got a   cou-ple of couch - es,   sleep on the love - seat.

Some-one keeps say-ing I'm in - sane to com-plain a - bout a   shot - gun wed-ding and a stain on my shirt.

tremolo off

Don't be - lieve ev -'ry-thing that you breathe. _ You get a park-ing vi - o - la - tion and a   mag-got on your sleeve. So

shave your face _ with some mace in the dark, _   sav-ing all your food stamps and burn-ing down the trail - er park.

N.C.

Yo.   Cut it.

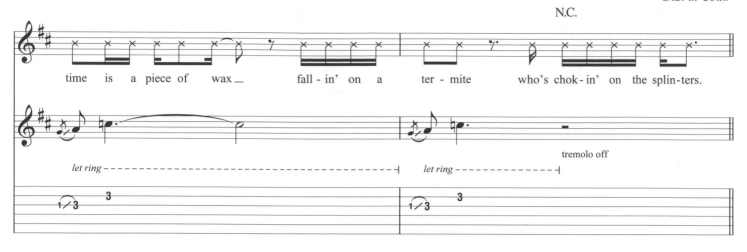

time is a piece of wax __ fall-in' on a ter - mite who's chok-in' on the splin-ters.

let ring — — — — — — — — — — — — —   *let ring* — — — — — — — — — tremolo off

Coda

Interlude
Gtr. tacet

__ don't you kill me? __

(Drive - by bod - y pierce.)

Yo, bring it on down. __

(Oy. __

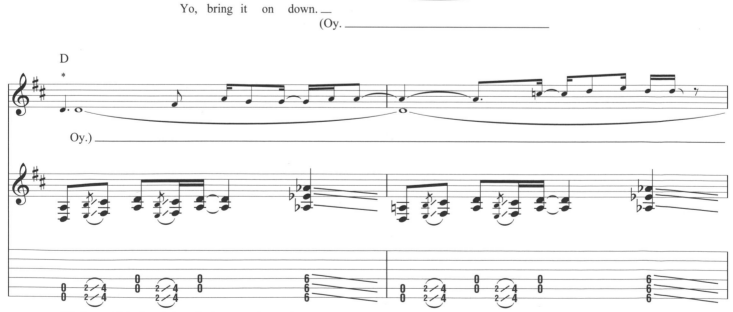

D

Oy.) __

*Upstem part is backward chorus lead voc. sample, next 4 meas.

Spoken: I'm a driver, I'm a winner.   Things are gonna change. I can feel it.

Chorus

Soy   un ___ per - de - dor. ___   I'm a

los - er, ba - by, ___   so why ___ don't you kill   me? ___
(I can't be - lieve ___ you.)
(And spre - chen Sie Deutsch - ie,

Outshined

Words and Music by Chris Cornell

Drop D tuning:
(low to high) D-A-D-G-B-E

Intro
Moderately slow Rock ♩ = 94

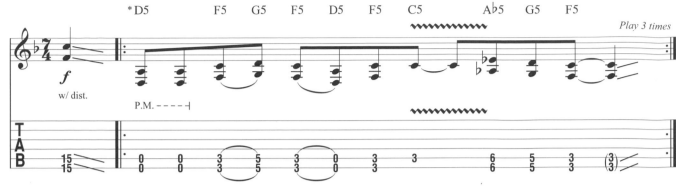

*Chord symbols reflect overall harmony.

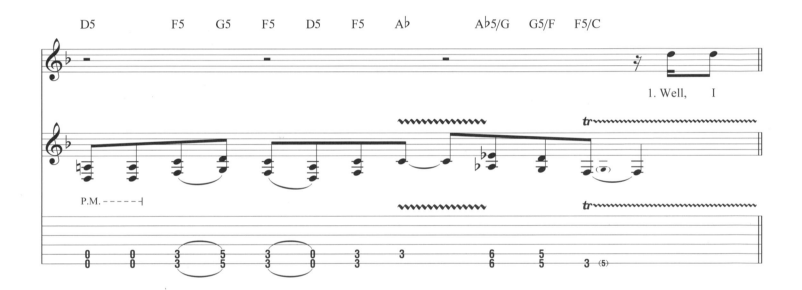

1. Well, I

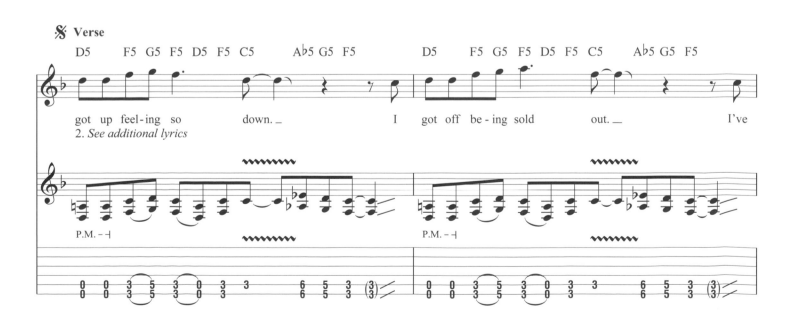

got up feel-ing so down. __ I got off be-ing sold out. __ I've
2. *See additional lyrics*

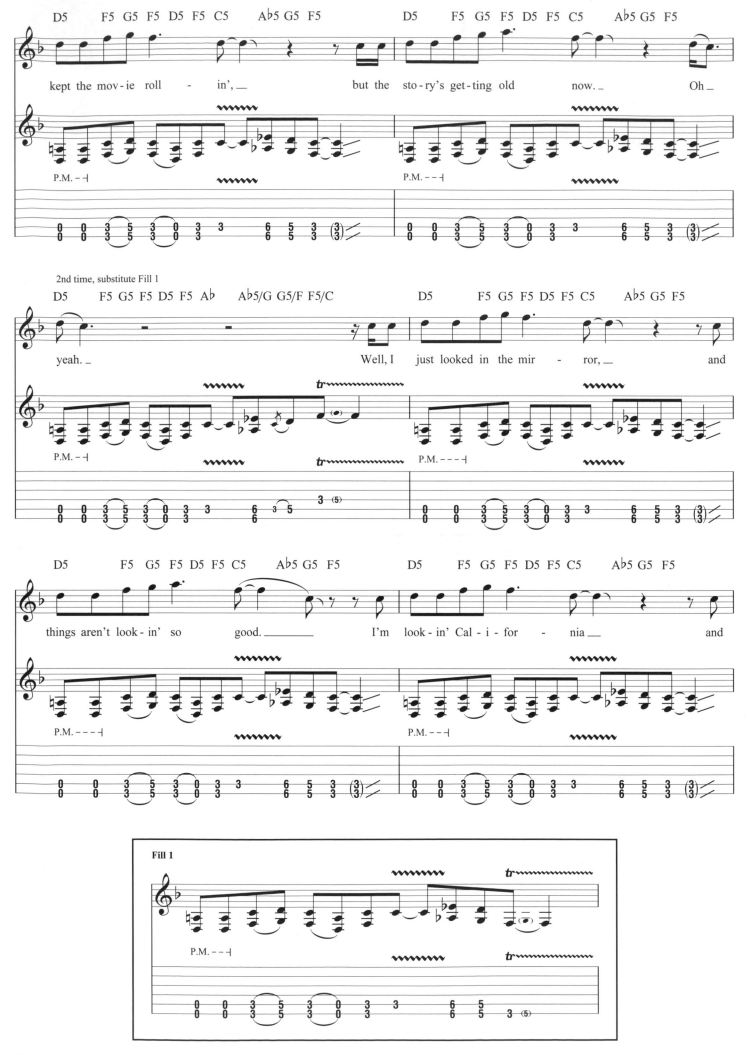

Interlude

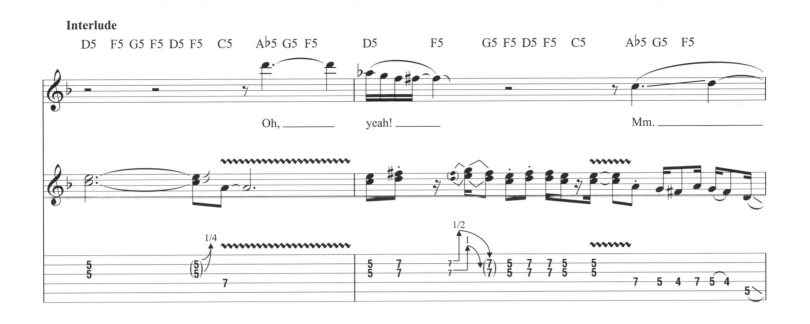

Oh, _____ yeah! _____

Mm. _____

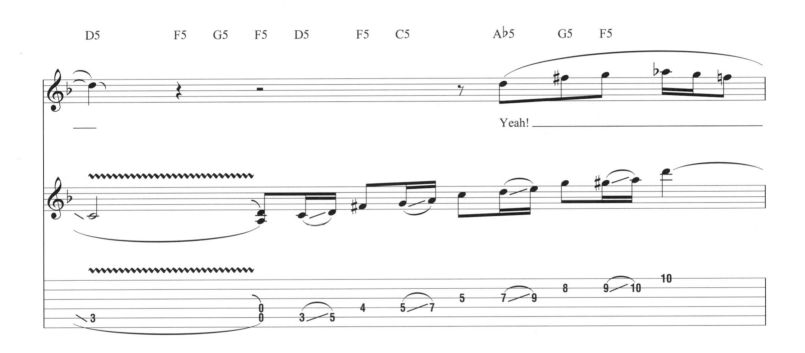

Yeah! _____

D.S. al Coda 1

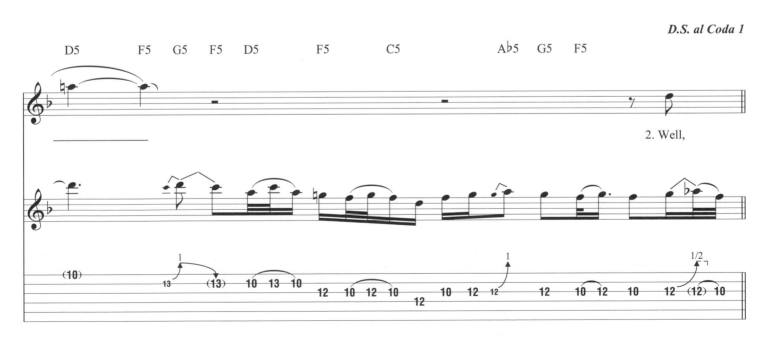

2. Well,

⊕ Coda 1

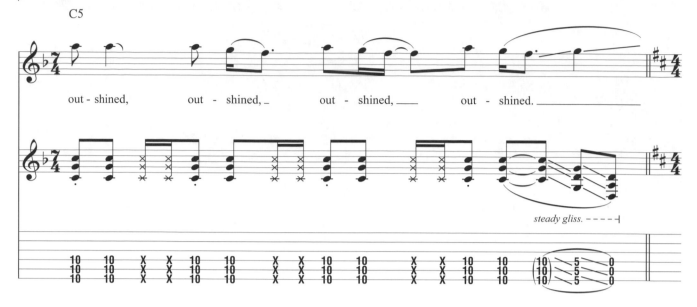

out - shined, out - shined, _ out - shined, ___ out - shined. _____

Interlude

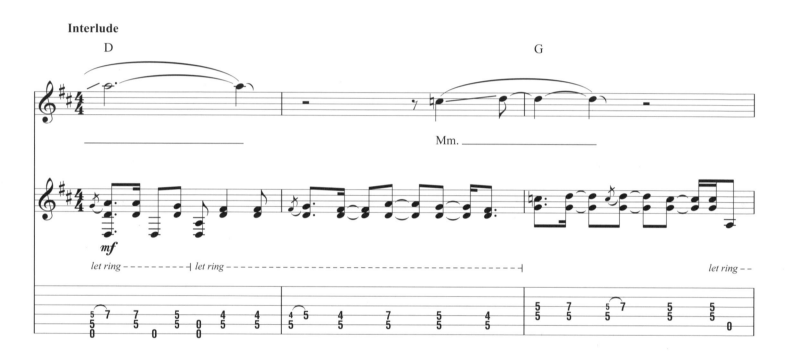

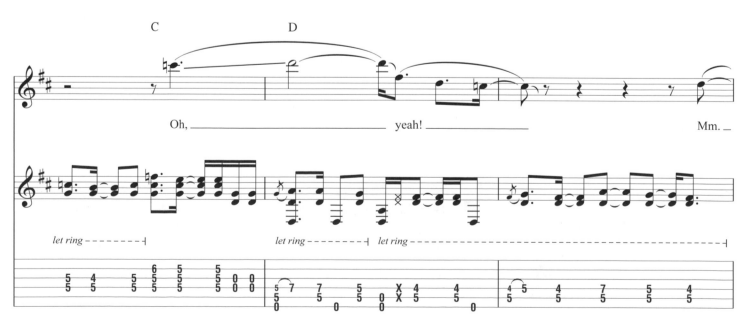

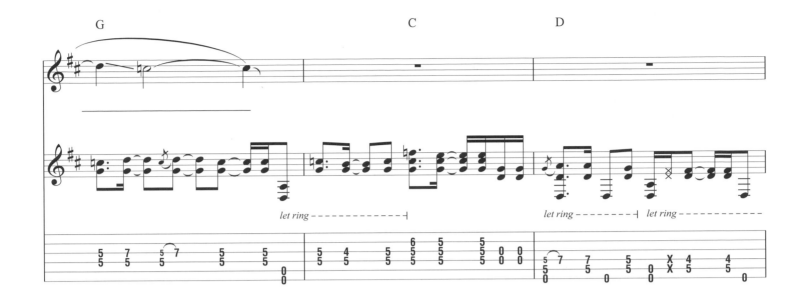

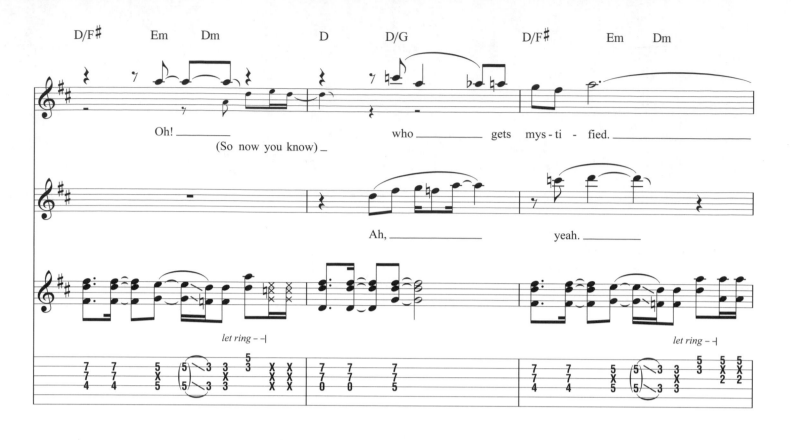

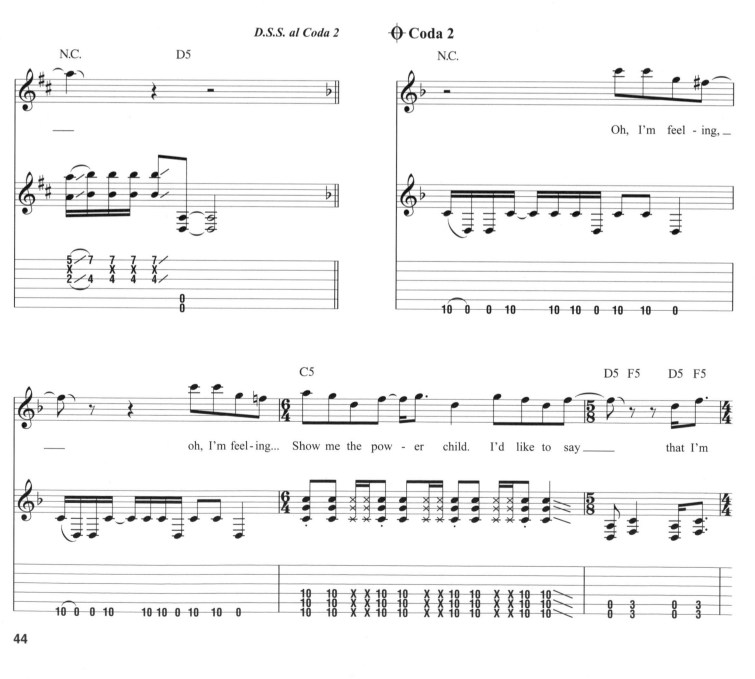

Additional Lyrics

2. Well, someone let the dogs out.
   They'll show you where the truth is.
   The grass is always greener
   Where the dogs are shitting. Oh, yeah.
   Well, I'm feeling that I'm sober,
   Even though I'm drinking.
   But I can't get any lower.
   Still I feel I'm sinking.

Man in the Box

Written by Jerry Cantrell and Layne Staley

Tune down 1/2 step:
(low to high) E♭-A♭-D♭-G♭-B♭-E♭

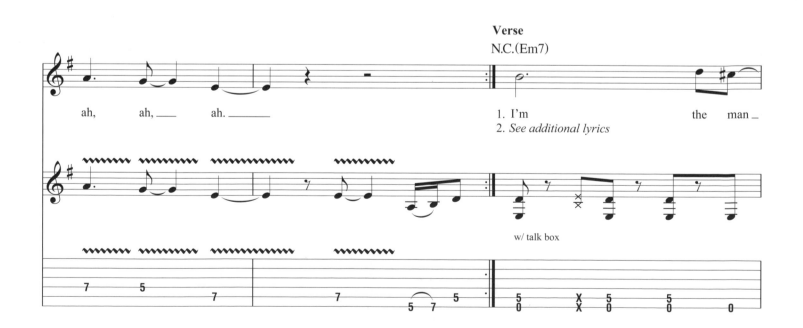

To Coda 1 ✛
To Coda 2 ✛
D.S. al Coda 1
(take repeat)

Coda 1

Guitar Solo

N.C.(Em7)

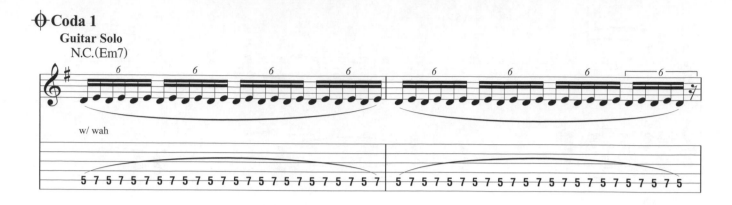

w/ wah

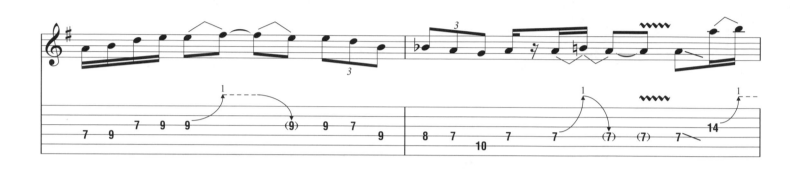

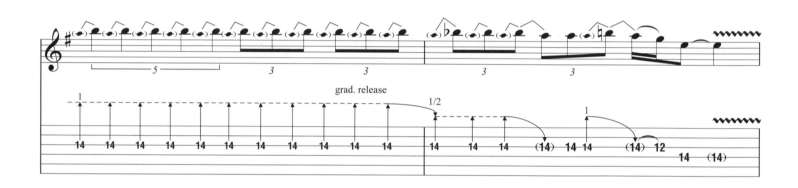

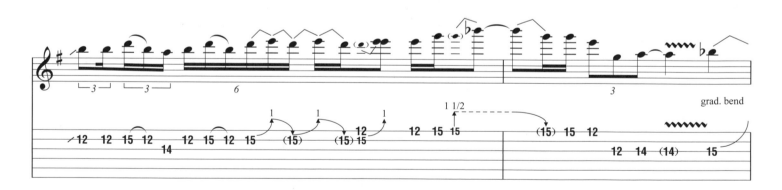

G

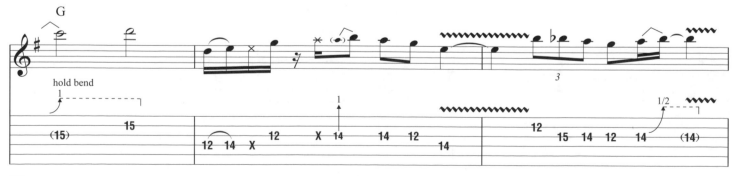

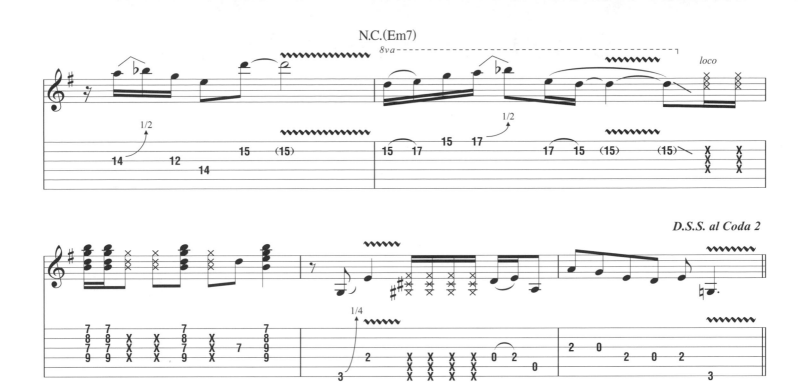

 Coda 2

Interlude

Ah, ah, ah, ah, ah, ah, ah, ah, ah.

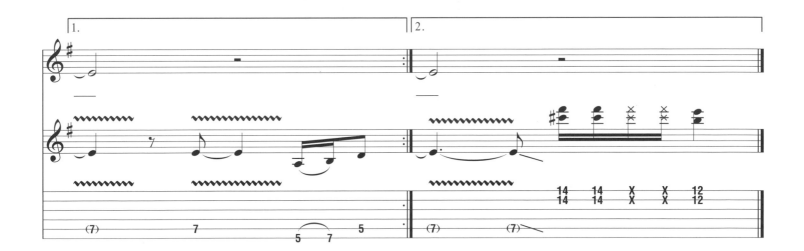

Additional Lyrics

2. I'm the dog who gets beat.
   Shove my nose in shit.

Smells Like Teen Spirit

Words and Music by Kurt Cobain, Krist Novoselic and Dave Grohl

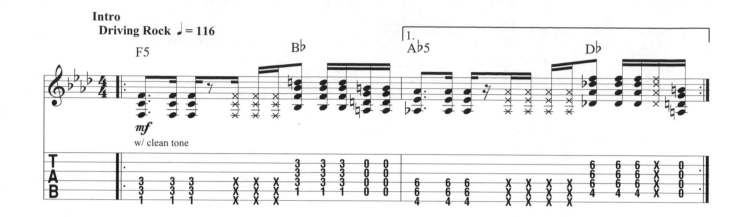

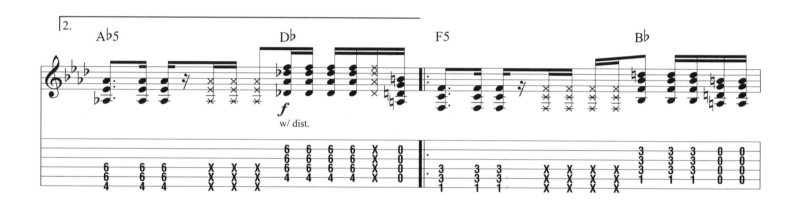

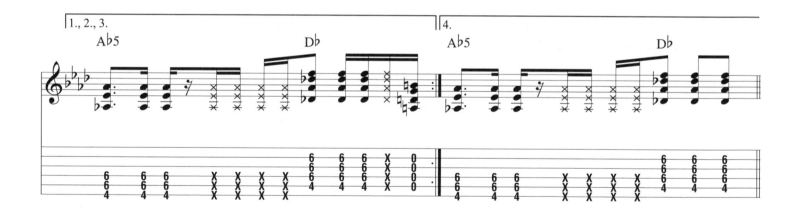

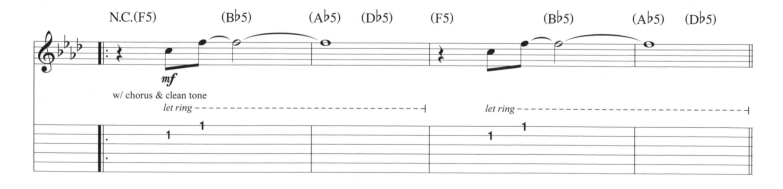

Verse

1. Load up ___ on guns ___ and bring ___ your friends. ___ It's fun ___ to lose ___
2. *See additional lyrics*

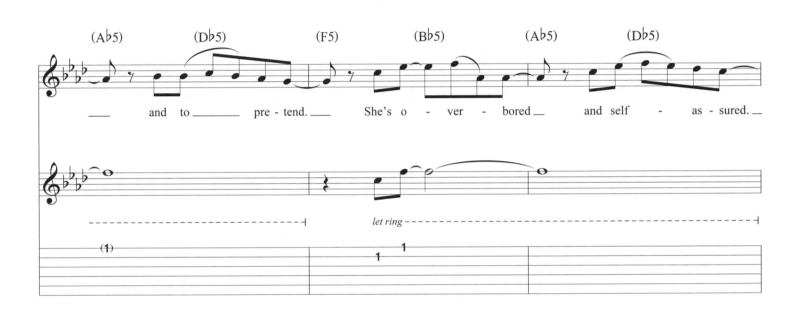

___ and to ___ pre - tend. ___ She's o - ver - bored ___ and self - as - sured. ___

Pre-Chorus

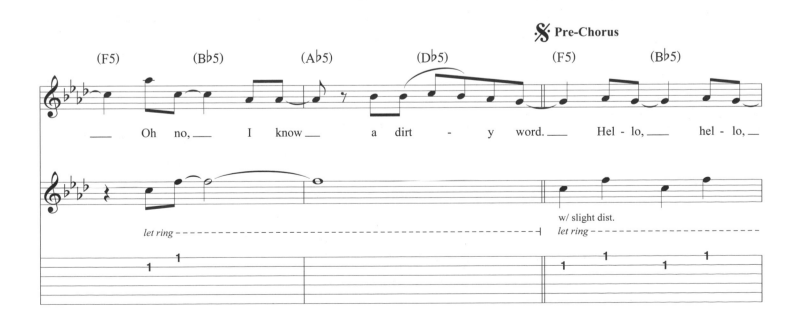

___ Oh no, ___ I know ___ a dirt - y word. ___ Hel - lo, ___ hel - lo, ___

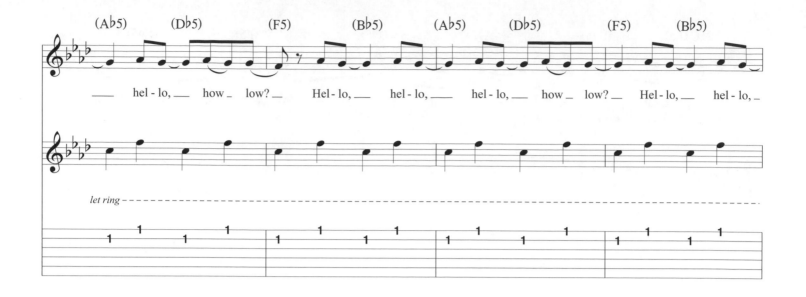

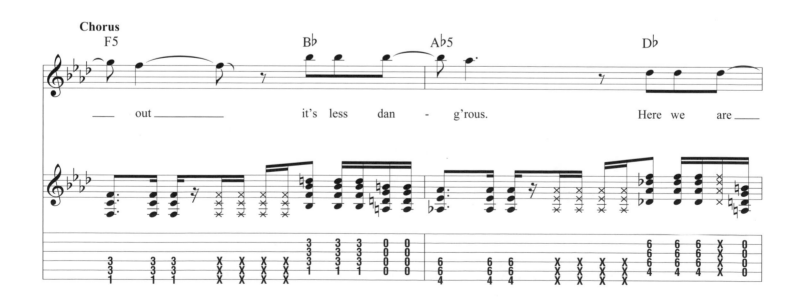

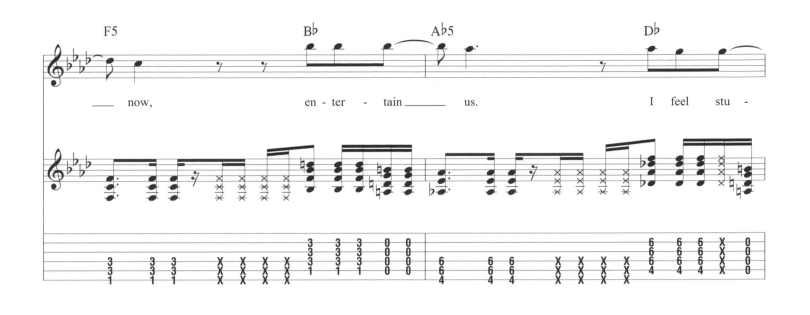

now, en - ter - tain _____ us. I feel stu -

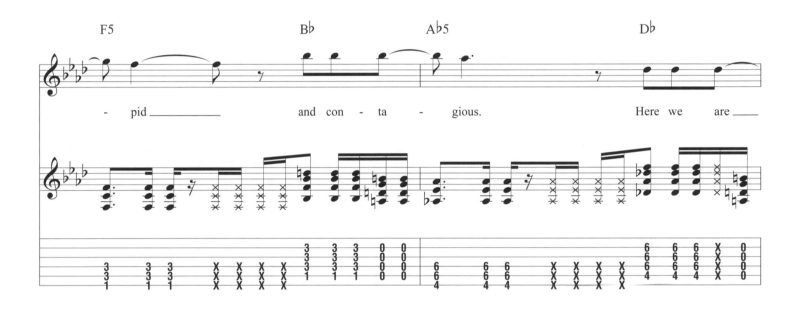

- pid _____ and con - ta - gious. Here we are _____

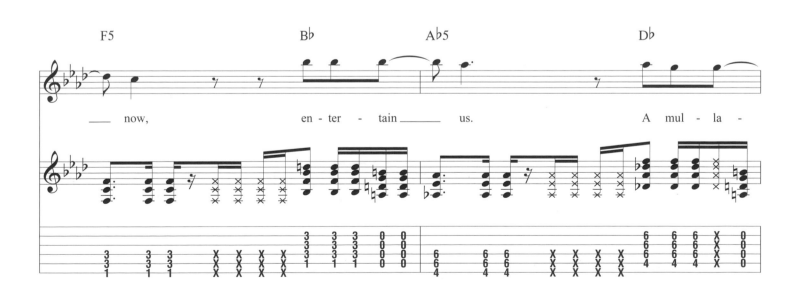

now, en - ter - tain _____ us. A mul - la -

- to, _____ an al - bi - no, a mos - qui -

To Coda ⊕

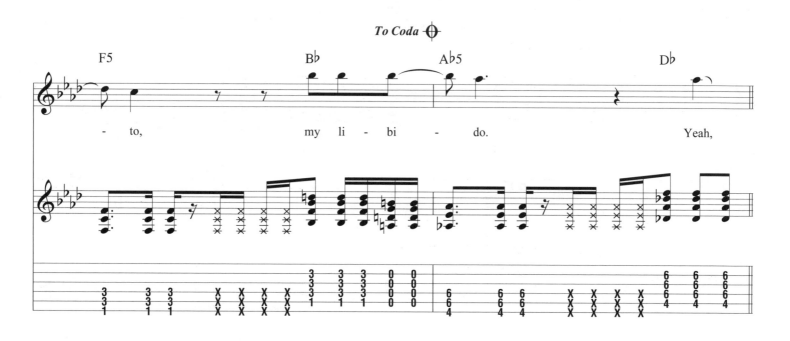

- to, my li - bi - do. Yeah,

Bridge

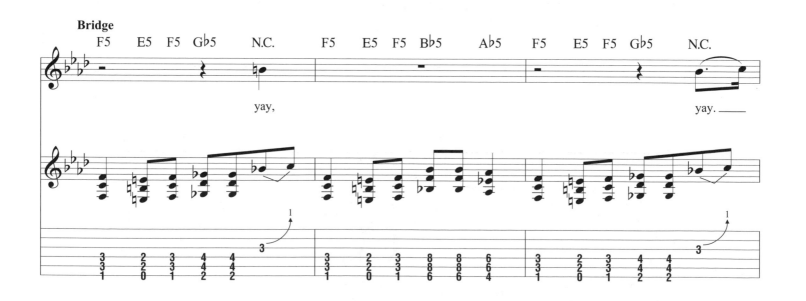

yay, yay. _____

Additional Lyrics

2. I'm worse at what I do best,
   And for this gift I feel blessed.
   Our little group has always been
   And always will until the end.

Under the Bridge

Words and Music by Anthony Kiedis, Flea, John Frusciante and Chad Smith

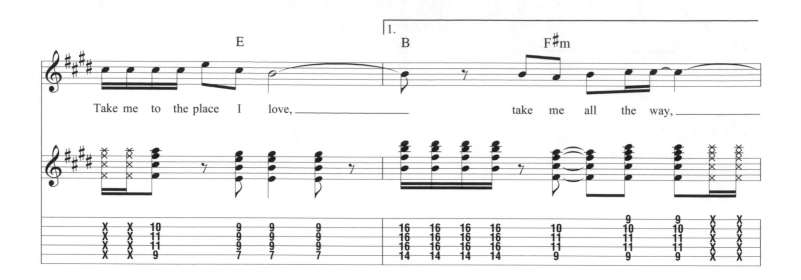

Take me to the place I love, _____ take me all the way, _____

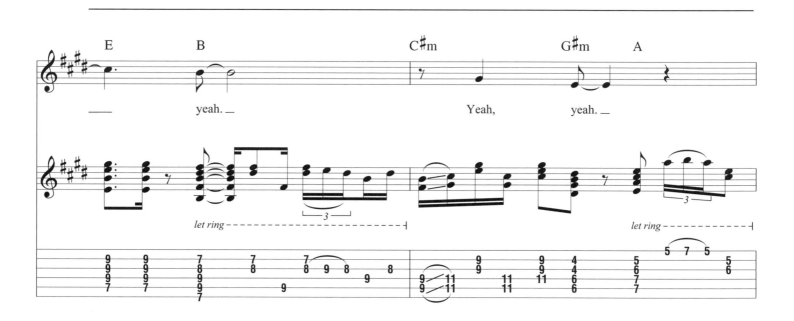

— yeah. ___ Yeah, yeah. ___

let ring - - - - - - - - - - - - - - - - -   let ring - - - - - - - - - -

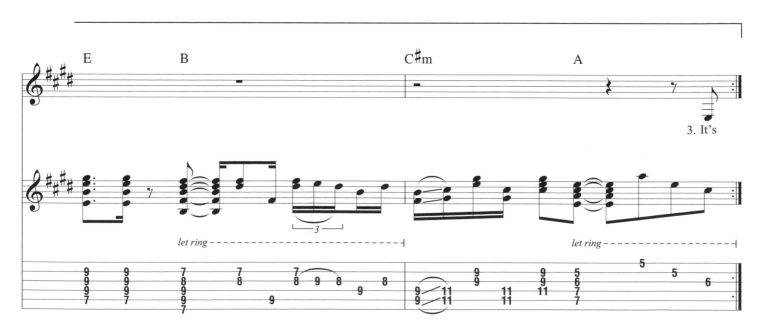

3. It's

let ring - - - - - - - - - - - - - -   let ring - - - - - - - - - -

(Un-der the bridge down - town.) _____

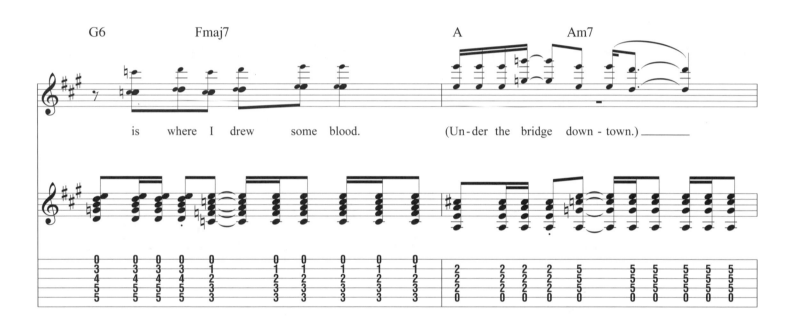

is where I drew some blood. (Un-der the bridge down - town.) _____

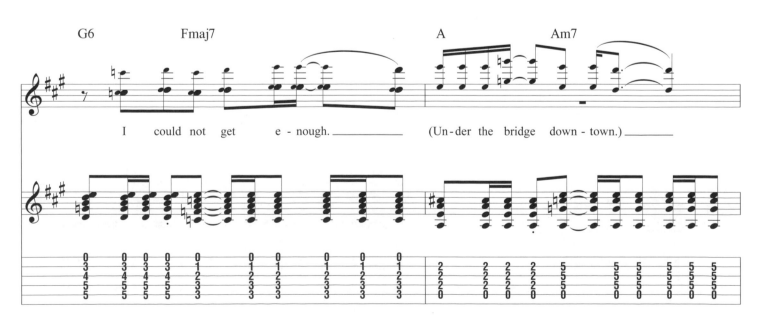

I could not get e - nough. _____ (Un-der the bridge down - town.) _____

for - got a - bout my love._____ (Un - der the bridge down - town.)_____

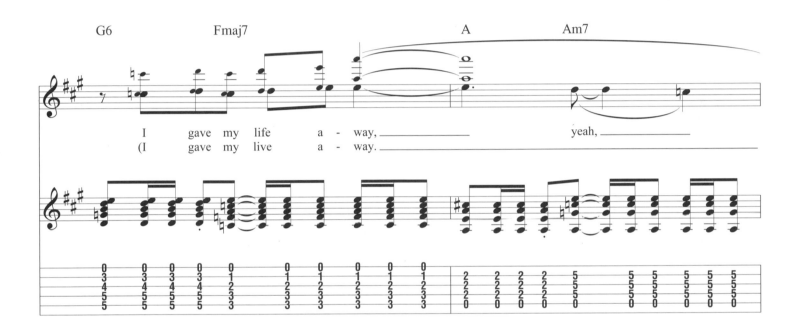

I gave my life a - way,_____ yeah,_____
(I gave my live a - way._____

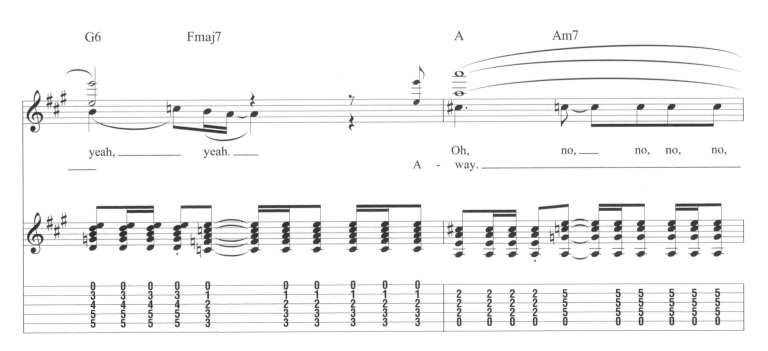

yeah,_____ yeah._____ Oh, no,____ no, no, no,
_____ A - way.

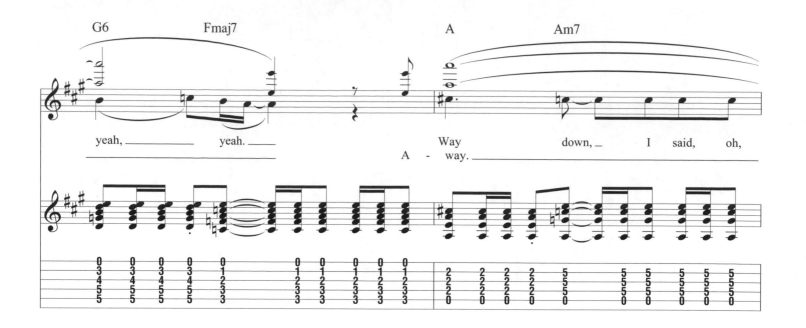

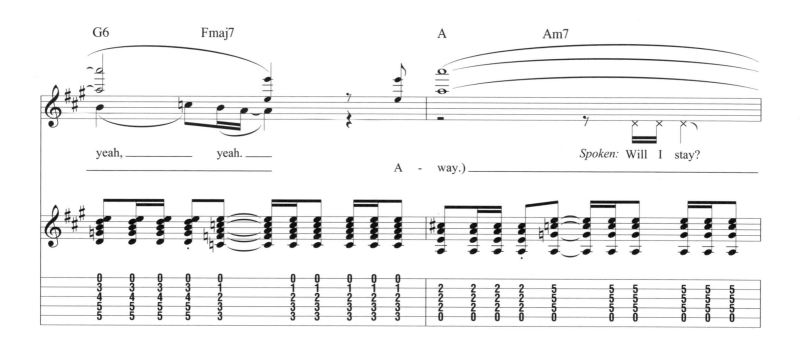

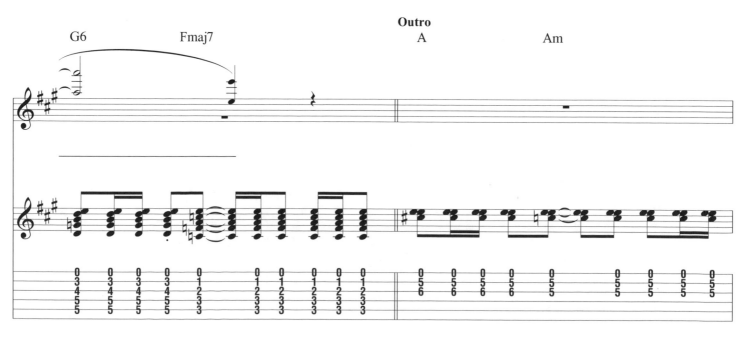

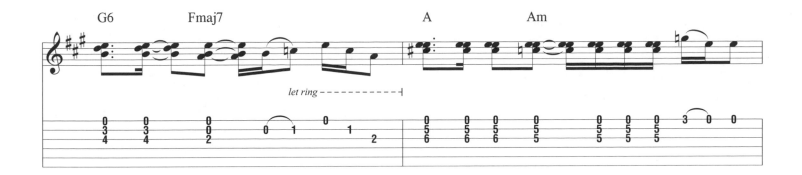

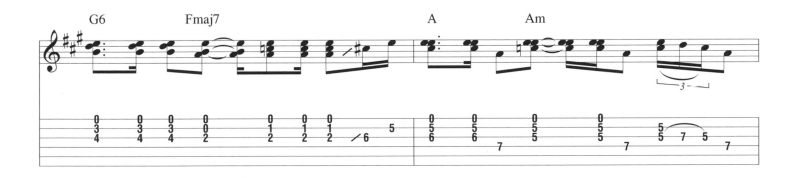

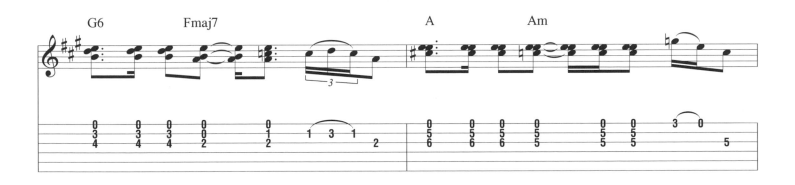

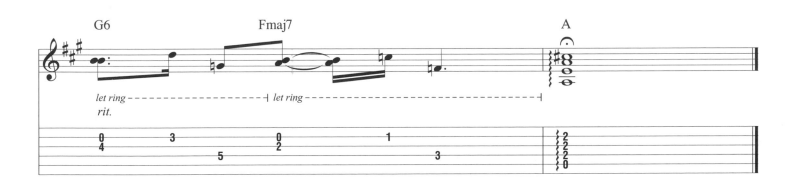

Additional Lyrics

3. It's hard to believe that there's nobody out there.
   It's hard to believe that I'm all alone.
   At least I have her love, the city, she loves me.
   Lonely as I am, together we cry.

HAL•LEONARD® GUITAR PLAY-ALONG

AUDIO ACCESS INCLUDED 🔊

This series will help you play your favorite songs quickly and easily. Just follow the tab and listen to the audio to the hear how the guitar should sound, and then play along using the separate backing tracks. Audio files also include software to slow down the tempo without changing pitch. The melody and lyrics are included in the book so that you can sing or simply follow along.

INCLUDES TAB

VOL. 1 – ROCK	00699570 / $16.99	
VOL. 2 – ACOUSTIC	00699569 / $16.99	
VOL. 3 – HARD ROCK	00699573 / $17.99	
VOL. 4 – POP/ROCK	00699571 / $16.99	
VOL. 6 – '90S ROCK	00699572 / $16.99	
VOL. 7 – BLUES	00699575 / $17.99	
VOL. 8 – ROCK	00699585 / $16.99	
VOL. 9 – EASY ACOUSTIC SONGS	00151708 / $16.99	
VOL. 10 – ACOUSTIC	00699586 / $16.95	
VOL. 13 – FOLK ROCK	00699581 / $16.99	
VOL. 14 – BLUES ROCK	00699582 / $16.99	
VOL. 15 – R&B	00699583 / $16.99	
VOL. 16 – JAZZ	00699584 / $15.95	
VOL. 17 – COUNTRY	00699588 / $16.99	
VOL. 18 – ACOUSTIC ROCK	00699577 / $15.95	
VOL. 20 – ROCKABILLY	00699580 / $16.99	
VOL. 21 – SANTANA	00174525 / $17.99	
VOL. 22 – CHRISTMAS	00699600 / $15.99	
VOL. 23 – SURF	00699635 / $15.99	
VOL. 24 – ERIC CLAPTON	00699649 / $17.99	
VOL. 25 – THE BEATLES	00198265 / $17.99	
VOL. 26 – ELVIS PRESLEY	00699643 / $16.99	
VOL. 27 – DAVID LEE ROTH	00699645 / $16.95	
VOL. 28 – GREG KOCH	00699646 / $17.99	
VOL. 29 – BOB SEGER	00699647 / $16.99	
VOL. 30 – KISS	00699644 / $16.99	
VOL. 32 – THE OFFSPRING	00699653 / $14.95	
VOL. 33 – ACOUSTIC CLASSICS	00699656 / $17.99	
VOL. 34 – CLASSIC ROCK	00699658 / $17.99	
VOL. 35 – HAIR METAL	00699660 / $17.99	
VOL. 36 – SOUTHERN ROCK	00699661 / $17.99	
VOL. 37 – ACOUSTIC UNPLUGGED	00699662 / $22.99	
VOL. 38 – BLUES	00699663 / $16.95	
VOL. 39 – '80S METAL	00699664 / $16.99	
VOL. 40 – INCUBUS	00699668 / $17.95	
VOL. 41 – ERIC CLAPTON	00699669 / $17.99	
VOL. 42 – COVER BAND HITS	00211597 / $16.99	
VOL. 43 – LYNYRD SKYNYRD	00699681 / $17.99	
VOL. 44 – JAZZ	00699689 / $16.99	
VOL. 45 – TV THEMES	00699718 / $14.95	
VOL. 46 – MAINSTREAM ROCK	00699722 / $16.95	
VOL. 47 – HENDRIX SMASH HITS	00699723 / $19.99	
VOL. 48 – AEROSMITH CLASSICS	00699724 / $17.99	
VOL. 49 – STEVIE RAY VAUGHAN	00699725 / $17.99	
VOL. 50 – VAN HALEN 1978-1984	00110269 / $17.99	
VOL. 51 – ALTERNATIVE '90S	00699727 / $14.99	
VOL. 52 – FUNK	00699728 / $15.99	
VOL. 53 – DISCO	00699729 / $14.99	
VOL. 54 – HEAVY METAL	00699730 / $16.99	
VOL. 55 – POP METAL	00699731 / $14.95	
VOL. 56 – FOO FIGHTERS	00699749 / $16.99	
VOL. 59 – CHET ATKINS	00702347 / $16.99	
VOL. 62 – CHRISTMAS CAROLS	00699798 / $12.95	
VOL. 63 – CREEDENCE CLEARWATER REVIVAL	00699802 / $16.99	
VOL. 64 – THE ULTIMATE OZZY OSBOURNE	00699803 / $17.99	
VOL. 66 – THE ROLLING STONES	00699807 / $17.99	
VOL. 67 – BLACK SABBATH	00699808 / $16.99	
VOL. 68 – PINK FLOYD – DARK SIDE OF THE MOON	00699809 / $16.99	
VOL. 70 – OZZY OSBOURNE	00699805 / $16.99	
VOL. 73 – BLUESY ROCK	00699829 / $16.99	
VOL. 74 – SIMPLE STRUMMING SONGS	00151706 / $19.99	

VOL. 75 – TOM PETTY	00699882 / $16.99
VOL. 76 – COUNTRY HITS	00699884 / $16.99
VOL. 77 – BLUEGRASS	00699910 / $15.99
VOL. 78 – NIRVANA	00700132 / $16.99
VOL. 79 – NEIL YOUNG	00700133 / $24.99
VOL. 80 – ACOUSTIC ANTHOLOGY	00700175 / $19.95
VOL. 81 – ROCK ANTHOLOGY	00700176 / $22.99
VOL. 82 – EASY SONGS	00700177 / $16.99
VOL. 84 – STEELY DAN	00700200 / $17.99
VOL. 85 – THE POLICE	00700269 / $16.99
VOL. 86 – BOSTON	00700465 / $16.99
VOL. 87 – ACOUSTIC WOMEN	00700763 / $14.99
VOL. 89 – REGGAE	00700468 / $15.99
VOL. 90 – CLASSICAL POP	00700469 / $14.99
VOL. 91 – BLUES INSTRUMENTALS	00700505 / $15.99
VOL. 92 – EARLY ROCK INSTRUMENTALS	00700506 / $15.99
VOL. 93 – ROCK INSTRUMENTALS	00700507 / $16.99
VOL. 94 – SLOW BLUES	00700508 / $16.99
VOL. 95 – BLUES CLASSICS	00700509 / $15.99
VOL. 96 – BEST COUNTRY HITS	00211615 / $16.99
VOL. 97 – CHRISTMAS CLASSICS	00236542 / $14.99
VOL. 99 – ZZ TOP	00700762 / $16.99
VOL. 100 – B.B. KING	00700466 / $16.99
VOL. 101 – SONGS FOR BEGINNERS	00701917 / $14.99
VOL. 102 – CLASSIC PUNK	00700769 / $14.99
VOL. 103 – SWITCHFOOT	00700773 / $16.99
VOL. 104 – DUANE ALLMAN	00700846 / $16.99
VOL. 105 – LATIN	00700939 / $16.99
VOL. 106 – WEEZER	00700958 / $14.99
VOL. 107 – CREAM	00701069 / $16.99
VOL. 108 – THE WHO	00701053 / $16.99
VOL. 109 – STEVE MILLER	00701054 / $19.99
VOL. 110 – SLIDE GUITAR HITS	00701055 / $16.99
VOL. 111 – JOHN MELLENCAMP	00701056 / $14.99
VOL. 112 – QUEEN	00701052 / $16.99
VOL. 113 – JIM CROCE	00701058 / $17.99
VOL. 114 – BON JOVI	00701060 / $16.99
VOL. 115 – JOHNNY CASH	00701070 / $16.99
VOL. 116 – THE VENTURES	00701124 / $16.99
VOL. 117 – BRAD PAISLEY	00701224 / $16.99
VOL. 118 – ERIC JOHNSON	00701353 / $16.99
VOL. 119 – AC/DC CLASSICS	00701356 / $17.99
VOL. 120 – PROGRESSIVE ROCK	00701457 / $14.99
VOL. 121 – U2	00701508 / $16.99
VOL. 122 – CROSBY, STILLS & NASH	00701610 / $16.99
VOL. 123 – LENNON & MCCARTNEY ACOUSTIC	00701614 / $16.99
VOL. 125 – JEFF BECK	00701687 / $16.99
VOL. 126 – BOB MARLEY	00701701 / $16.99
VOL. 127 – 1970S ROCK	00701739 / $16.99
VOL. 128 – 1960S ROCK	00701740 / $14.99
VOL. 129 – MEGADETH	00701741 / $17.99
VOL. 130 – IRON MAIDEN	00701742 / $17.99
VOL. 131 – 1990S ROCK	00701743 / $14.99
VOL. 132 – COUNTRY ROCK	00701757 / $15.99
VOL. 133 – TAYLOR SWIFT	00701894 / $16.99
VOL. 134 – AVENGED SEVENFOLD	00701906 / $16.99
VOL. 135 – MINOR BLUES	0151350 / $17.99
VOL. 136 – GUITAR THEMES	00701922 / $14.99
VOL. 137 – IRISH TUNES	00701966 / $15.99
VOL. 138 – BLUEGRASS CLASSICS	00701967 / $16.99
VOL. 139 – GARY MOORE	00702370 / $16.99
VOL. 140 – MORE STEVIE RAY VAUGHAN	00702396 / $17.99
VOL. 141 – ACOUSTIC HITS	00702401 / $16.99

VOL. 142 – GEORGE HARRISON	00237697 / $17.99
VOL. 143 – SLASH	00702425 / $19.99
VOL. 144 – DJANGO REINHARDT	00702531 / $16.99
VOL. 145 – DEF LEPPARD	00702532 / $17.99
VOL. 146 – ROBERT JOHNSON	00702533 / $16.99
VOL. 147 – SIMON & GARFUNKEL	14041591 / $16.99
VOL. 148 – BOB DYLAN	14041592 / $16.99
VOL. 149 – AC/DC HITS	14041593 / $17.99
VOL. 150 – ZAKK WYLDE	02501717 / $16.99
VOL. 151 – J.S. BACH	02501730 / $16.99
VOL. 152 – JOE BONAMASSA	02501751 / $19.99
VOL. 153 – RED HOT CHILI PEPPERS	00702990 / $19.99
VOL. 155 – ERIC CLAPTON – FROM THE ALBUM UNPLUGGED	00703085 / $16.99
VOL. 156 – SLAYER	00703770 / $17.99
VOL. 157 – FLEETWOOD MAC	00101382 / $16.99
VOL. 159 – WES MONTGOMERY	00102593 / $19.99
VOL. 160 – T-BONE WALKER	00102641 / $17.99
VOL. 161 – THE EAGLES – ACOUSTIC	00102659 / $17.99
VOL. 162 – THE EAGLES HITS	00102667 / $17.99
VOL. 163 – PANTERA	00103036 / $17.99
VOL. 164 – VAN HALEN 1986-1995	00110270 / $17.99
VOL. 165 – GREEN DAY	00210343 / $17.99
VOL. 166 – MODERN BLUES	00700764 / $16.99
VOL. 167 – DREAM THEATER	00111938 / $24.99
VOL. 168 – KISS	00113421 / $17.99
VOL. 169 – TAYLOR SWIFT	00115982 / $16.99
VOL. 170 – THREE DAYS GRACE	00117337 / $16.99
VOL. 171 – JAMES BROWN	00117420 / $16.99
VOL. 172 – THE DOOBIE BROTHERS	00119670 / $16.99
VOL. 173 – TRANS-SIBERIAN ORCHESTRA	00119907 / $19.99
VOL. 174 – SCORPIONS	00122119 / $16.99
VOL. 175 – MICHAEL SCHENKER	00122127 / $16.99
VOL. 176 – BLUES BREAKERS WITH JOHN MAYALL & ERIC CLAPTON	00122132 / $19.99
VOL. 177 – ALBERT KING	00123271 / $16.99
VOL. 178 – JASON MRAZ	00124165 / $17.99
VOL. 179 – RAMONES	00127073 / $16.99
VOL. 180 – BRUNO MARS	00129706 / $16.99
VOL. 181 – JACK JOHNSON	00129854 / $16.99
VOL. 182 – SOUNDGARDEN	00138161 / $17.99
VOL. 183 – BUDDY GUY	00138240 / $17.99
VOL. 184 – KENNY WAYNE SHEPHERD	00138258 / $17.99
VOL. 185 – JOE SATRIANI	00139457 / $17.99
VOL. 186 – GRATEFUL DEAD	00139459 / $17.99
VOL. 187 – JOHN DENVER	00140839 / $17.99
VOL. 188 – MÖTLEY CRUE	00141145 / $17.99
VOL. 189 – JOHN MAYER	00144350 / $17.99
VOL. 190 – DEEP PURPLE	00146152 / $17.99
VOL. 191 – PINK FLOYD CLASSICS	00146164 / $17.99
VOL. 192 – JUDAS PRIEST	00151352 / $17.99
VOL. 193 – STEVE VAI	00156028 / $19.99
VOL. 195 – METALLICA: 1983-1988	00234291 / $19.99
VOL. 196 – METALLICA: 1991-2016	00234292 / $19.99

Prices, contents, and availability subject to change without notice.

Complete song lists available online.

HAL•LEONARD®
www.halleonard.com

0319
173

RECORDED VERSIONS®
The Best Note-For-Note Transcriptions Available

AUTHENTIC TRANSCRIPTIONS WITH NOTES AND TABLATURE

COMPLETE SERIES LIST ONLINE!

HAL•LEONARD®
www.halleonard.com

Prices and availability subject to change without notice.
*Tab transcriptions only.

GUITAR *signature licks*

Signature Licks book/audio packs provide a step-by-step breakdown of "right from the record" riffs, licks, and solos so you can jam along with your favorite bands. They contain performance notes and an overview of each artist's or group's style, with note-for-note transcriptions in notes and tab. The CDs or online audio tracks feature full-band demos at both normal and slow speeds.

AC/DC
14041352......................$22.99

AEROSMITH 1973-1979
00695106......................$22.95

AEROSMITH 1979-1998
00695219......................$22.95

DUANE ALLMAN
00696042......................$22.99

BEST OF CHET ATKINS
00695752......................$24.99

AVENGED SEVENFOLD
00696473......................$22.99

BEST OF THE BEATLES FOR ACOUSTIC GUITAR
00695453......................$22.99

THE BEATLES BASS
00695283......................$22.99

THE BEATLES FAVORITES
00695096......................$24.95

THE BEATLES HITS
00695049......................$24.95

JEFF BECK
00696427......................$22.99

BEST OF GEORGE BENSON
00695418......................$22.99

BEST OF BLACK SABBATH
00695249......................$22.95

BLUES BREAKERS WITH JOHN MAYALL & ERIC CLAPTON
00696374......................$22.99

BON JOVI
00696380......................$22.99

ROY BUCHANAN
00696654......................$22.99

KENNY BURRELL
00695830......................$24.99

BEST OF CHARLIE CHRISTIAN
00695584......................$22.95

BEST OF ERIC CLAPTON
00695038......................$24.99

ERIC CLAPTON – FROM THE ALBUM UNPLUGGED
00695250......................$24.95

BEST OF CREAM
00695251......................$22.95

CREEDANCE CLEARWATER REVIVAL
00695924......................$22.95

DEEP PURPLE – GREATEST HITS
00695625......................$22.99

THE BEST OF DEF LEPPARD
00696516......................$22.99

DREAM THEATER
00111943......................$24.99

TOMMY EMMANUEL
00696409......................$22.99

ESSENTIAL JAZZ GUITAR
00695875......................$19.99

FAMOUS ROCK GUITAR SOLOS
00695590......................$19.95

FLEETWOOD MAC
00696416......................$22.99

BEST OF FOO FIGHTERS
00695481......................$24.95

ROBBEN FORD
00695903......................$22.95

BEST OF GRANT GREEN
00695747......................$22.99

PETER GREEN
00145386......................$22.99

THE GUITARS OF ELVIS – 2ND ED.
00174800......................$22.99

BEST OF GUNS N' ROSES
00695183......................$24.99

THE BEST OF BUDDY GUY
00695186......................$22.99

JIM HALL
00695848......................$24.99

JIMI HENDRIX
00696560......................$24.99

JIMI HENDRIX – VOLUME 2
00695835......................$24.99

JOHN LEE HOOKER
00695894......................$19.99

BEST OF JAZZ GUITAR
00695586......................$24.95

ERIC JOHNSON
00699317......................$24.99

ROBERT JOHNSON
00695264......................$22.95

BARNEY KESSEL
00696009......................$24.99

THE ESSENTIAL ALBERT KING
00695713......................$22.95

B.B. KING – BLUES LEGEND
00696039......................$22.99

B.B. KING – THE DEFINITIVE COLLECTION
00695635......................$22.95

B.B. KING – MASTER BLUESMAN
00699923......................$24.99

MARK KNOPFLER
00695178......................$24.99

LYNYRD SKYNYRD
00695872......................$24.99

THE BEST OF YNGWIE MALMSTEEN
00695669......................$22.95

BEST OF PAT MARTINO
00695632......................$24.99

MEGADETH
00696421......................$22.99

WES MONTGOMERY
00695387......................$24.99

BEST OF NIRVANA
00695483......................$24.95

VERY BEST OF OZZY OSBOURNE
00695431......................$22.99

BRAD PAISLEY
00696379......................$22.99

BEST OF JOE PASS
00695730......................$22.99

JACO PASTORIUS
00695544......................$24.95

TOM PETTY
00696021......................$22.99

PINK FLOYD
00103659......................$24.99

BEST OF QUEEN
00695097......................$24.99

RADIOHEAD
00109304......................$24.99

BEST OF RAGE AGAINST THE MACHINE
00695480......................$24.95

RED HOT CHILI PEPPERS
00695173......................$22.95

RED HOT CHILI PEPPERS – GREATEST HITS
00695828......................$24.99

JERRY REED
00118236......................$22.99

BEST OF DJANGO REINHARDT
00695660......................$24.99

BEST OF ROCK 'N' ROLL GUITAR
00695559......................$22.99

BEST OF ROCKABILLY GUITAR
00695785......................$19.95

BEST OF CARLOS SANTANA
00174664......................$22.99

BEST OF JOE SATRIANI
00695216......................$22.95

SLASH
00696576......................$22.99

SLAYER
00121281......................$22.99

THE BEST OF SOUL GUITAR
00695703......................$19.95

BEST OF SOUTHERN ROCK
00695560......................$19.95

STEELY DAN
00696015......................$22.99

MIKE STERN
00695800......................$24.99

BEST OF SURF GUITAR
00695822......................$19.99

STEVE VAI
00673247......................$22.95

STEVE VAI – ALIEN LOVE SECRETS: THE NAKED VAMPS
00695223......................$22.95

STEVE VAI – FIRE GARDEN: THE NAKED VAMPS
00695166......................$22.95

STEVE VAI – THE ULTRA ZONE: NAKED VAMPS
00695684......................$22.95

VAN HALEN
00110227......................$24.99

STEVIE RAY VAUGHAN – 2ND ED.
00699316......................$24.95

THE GUITAR STYLE OF STEVIE RAY VAUGHAN
00695155......................$24.95

BEST OF THE VENTURES
00695772......................$19.95

THE WHO – 2ND ED.
00695561......................$22.95

JOHNNY WINTER
00695951......................$22.99

YES
00113120......................$22.99

NEIL YOUNG – GREATEST HITS
00695988......................$22.99

BEST OF ZZ TOP
00695738......................$24.95

HAL•LEONARD®

www.halleonard.com

COMPLETE DESCRIPTIONS AND SONGLISTS ONLINE!
Prices, contents and availability subject to change without notice.